The Movie Trivia Book

by Mel Simons

Also by Mel Simons:

The Old-Time Radio Trivia Book
The Old-Time Television Trivia Book
Old-Time Radio Memories
The Show-Biz Trivia Book
Old-Time Television Memories

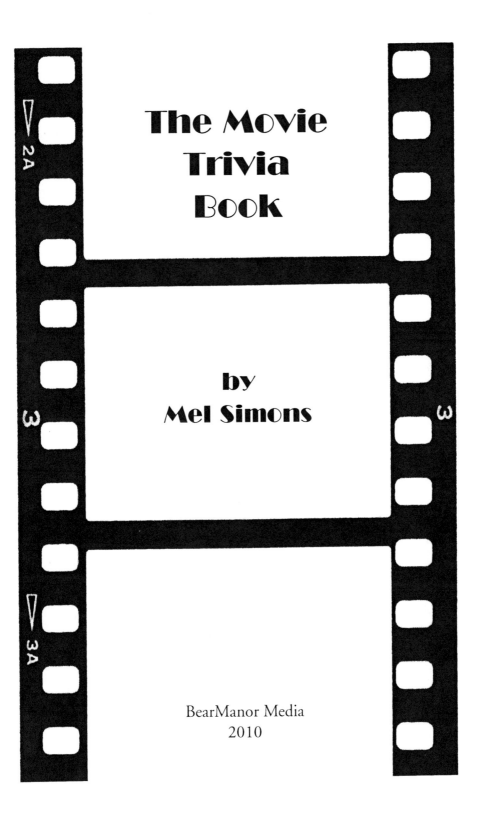

The Movie Trivia Book

by
Mel Simons

BearManor Media
2010

The Movie Trivia Book

Copyright © 2010 by Mel Simons

For information, address:

BearManor Media
P. O. Box 71426
Albany, GA 31708

bearmanormedia.com

Cover design by John Teehan
Typesetting and layout by John Teehan

ISBN—1-59393-518-8

Dedication

This book is dedicated to my grandnephew,

Judah Goldman

Mel Simons

Acknowledgements

Steve LeVeille—WBZ Radio Talk Show host in Boston. I've been a regular on his show for ten years. It's been a blast. Steve is the best thing about Boston radio.

Rex Trailer—Boston Television Icon. I am a long-time fan. Thanks for writing a great Foreword.

Henry Levin—I greatly appreciate the unlimited access you gave me to your copier.

Foreword

Howdy Folks! I'm Rex Trailer. Welcome to BOOMTOWN. Our TRIVIA question for today is—

Who's Mel Simons?

OK, OK, I know. I told you he's a friend of mine, and that he's written lots of books on all sorts of TRIVIA, and that he appears on TV and Radio telling people about trivia and asking questions, and if their answer is right they get a prize, but there's more about Mel Simons than that!

Did you know that he's an entertainer and a musician, he's been on the stage, he's a singer, a Master of Ceremonies, and a humorist?

On top of all that, he is a writer who writes those great books on all sorts of trivia: old-time radio, show biz trivia, old-time television, and trivia about things that are going on in entertainment these days.

And now he has just written this new book and you're in for a treat.

Sooooooo—the trvia question today is—-

Who's Mel Simons?????

OOPS!! I think I just gave the answer away.

– Rex Trailer

Quiz #1

GENERAL QUESTIONS

(Answers on page 101)

1. Name the rival street gangs in the movie *West Side Story*.

2. Who composed the music from *Shaft?*

3. What were the last names of Bonnie and Clyde?

4. What was the name of the first Cinerama movie?

5. What is Indian Jones' first name?

6. Ben Kingsley won the Oscar for which movie?

7. Who was known as "The Vamp?"

8. What is the name of Blondie's dog?

9. Name the biggest grossing film of all time.

10. Broderick Crawford played what character in *All The King's Men?*

Humphrey Bogart

Quiz #2

HUMPHREY BOGART

(Answers on page 101)

1. Bogie's last marriage was to whom?

2. What branch of service was Bogie in during World War I?

3. He won the Academy Award as Best Actor in which movie?

4. In *Sabrina*, who was his co-star?

5. Name the private eye he plays in *The Big Sleep*.

6. What was Bogie's last movie?

7. His last movie was loosely based on the life of whom?

8. He starred with James Cagney and Pat O'Brien in which film?

9. Who directed *The Treasure of Sierra Madre?*

10. Bogie was the leader of what social group that consisted of his drinking buddies?

Quiz #3

MULTIPLE CHOICE

(Answers on page 102)

1. The movie *Orchestra Wives* featured what big band?
    a) Harry James   b) Tommy Dorsey   c) Glen Miller

2. Gene Autry owned which baseball team?
    a) Detroit Tigers   b) California Angels   c) Chicago Cubs

3. The movie *Madame X* starred whom?
    a) Grace Kelly   b) Lana Turner   c) Ann Sheridan

4. Alice Faye was married to whom?
    a) Phil Harris   b) Tony Martin   c) Louis Jordan

5. Where was Cary Grand born?
    a) England   b) Scotland   c) Brussels

6. What musical instrument did Jerry Colona play?
    a) Trombone   b) Trumpet   c) Harp

7. Who played the wizard in *The Wizard of Oz?*
    a) Ed Wynn   b) Keenan Wynn   c) Frank Morgan

8. In the movie *The Great White Hope,* James Earl Jones played what boxer?
    a) Jack Johnson   b) Ray Robinson   c) Marvin Hagler

9. Who was known as "The Great Stone Face?"
    a) Boris Karloff   b) Buster Keaton   c) Peter Lorre

10. Orson Welles once did a commercial for what wine company?
    a) Carlo Rossi   b) Gallo   c) Paul Maisson

Quiz #4

CARTOONS

(Answers on page 102)

1. Which cartoon character would always say "Thuffering thuccotash?"

2. Who was Popeye's number one villain?

3. Name the well-known panda.

4. What cartoon girl used to advertise Kleenex Tissues?

5. Who starred in *The Incredible Mr. Limpet?*

6. Name Donald Duck's nephews.

7. What kind of an animal was Felix?

8. Who created Tom and Jerry for MGM?

9. Mickey Mouse had a girl friend. What was her name?

10. What was Bugs Bunny's favorite food?

Lana Turner

Quiz #5

MATCH THE SONG WITH THE MOVIE

(Answers on page 102)

1. "Thumbelina"
2. "Evergreen"
3. "That's Amore"
4. "Lullabye of Broadway"
5. "When You Wish Upon a Star"
6. "True Love"
7. "What a Feeling"
8. "I've Had the Time of My Life"
9. "Count Your Blessings"
10. "Say You, Say Me"

a. Pinocchio
b. Flashdance
c. Dirty Dancing
d. The Caddy
e. White Knight
f. Hans Christian Anderson
g. White Christmas
h. A Star Is Born
i. High Society
j. Gold Diggers of 1935

Quiz #6

HOLIDAY MOVIES

(Answers on page 103)

1. Bing Crosby sang the song "White Christmas" in what two movies?

2. Who won the Oscar for Best Supporting Actor in *Going My Way?*

3. *It's a Wonderful Life* starred which actor?

4. Who wrote the movie *The Christmas Story?*

5. Name the child star in the movie *Miracle On 34th Street.*

6. The song "Silver Bells" is from which movie?

7. Who starred in *Dr. Seuss' How the Grinch Stole Christmas?*

8. *The Bells of St. Mary* was the sequel to which movie?

9. The song *"We Need a Little Christmas"* is sung in what movie?

10. Who sang the song "Frosty, the Snowman" in the movie of the same name?

Quiz #7

WESTERN MOVIES

(Answers on page 103)

1. High Noon
2. Cat Ballou
3. Four For Texas
4. Shane
5. One-Eyed Jacks
6. Bad Day at Black Rock
7. Little Big Man
8. The Sons of Katie Elder
9. The Magnificent Seven
10. Butch Cassidy and the Sundance Kid

a. Alan Ladd
b. Gary Cooper
c. Spencer Tracy
d. John Wayne
e. Lee Marvin
f. Dustin Hoffman
g. Yul Brynner
h. Marlon Brando
i. Frank Sinatra
j. Robert Redford

Quiz #8

GENERAL QUESTIONS

(Answers on page 103)

1. Who has won the most Oscars for Best Supporting Actor?

2. Jack Albertson is married to whom in *The Poseidon Adventure?*

3. The movie *Sorry, Wrong Number* was originally done on a radio show. Name the radio show.

4. Who was the star of the movie?

5. What was Ronald Reagan's last movie?

6. Who was the first centerfold for Playboy Magazine?

7. In the movie, *An Officer and a Gentleman*, who played the drill instructor?

8. Name the two stars of *Midnight Cowboy.*

9. Sally Field starred in what 1970s television show?

10. Where was Frank Sinatra born?

Quiz #9

FILM DIRECTORS

Match the movie with the director.

(Answers on page 104)

1. *The Godfather*
2. *Dances With Wolves*
3. *Ben-Hur*
4. *It's a Wonderful Life*
5. *Caberet*
6. *The Graduate*
7. *The Greatest Show on Earth*
8. *Braveheart*
9. *A Clockwork Orange*
10. *My Fair Lady*

a. Mike Nichols
b. Frank Capra
c. Cecil B. DeMille
d. Kevin Costner
e. Francis Ford Coppola
f. Mel Gibson
g. William Wyler
h. Bob Fosse
i. George Cukar
j. Stanley Kubrick

Alfred Hitchcock

Quiz #10

ALFRED HITCHCOCK

(Answers on page 104)

1. What was Hitchcock's biggest-grossing movie?

2. Name the only Hitchcock film to win the Academy Award for best picture.

3. What was his nickname?

4. Jimmy Stewart witnesses a murder in what movie?

5. *The Man Who Knew Too Much* won the Oscar for what song?

6. Name the two stars in *Spellbound*.

7. In 1967, the Academy of Motion Picture Arts and Science awarded Hitchcock with what?

8. Name the three Hitchcock movies that starred Grace Kelly.

9. What was the name of his popular television show?

10. Name the Hitchcock movie that starred Cary Grant and Joan Fontaine.

Quiz #11

REAL NAMES

Match the actress with her real name.

(Answers on page 104)

1. Cher
2. Joan Crawford
3. Jean Harlow
4. Ellen Burstyn
5. Gloria Swanson
6. Cyd Charisse
7. Anne Bancroft
8. Lee Grant
9. Ann Sothern
10. Piper Laurie

a. Harriette Lake
b. Rosetta Jacobs
c. Edna Rae Gillooly
d. Lucille Chauchoin
e. Tula Ellice Finklea
f. Josephine Swenson
g. Cherilyn Sarkasian
h. Anna Maria Louisa Italiano
i. Lyova Rosenthal
j. Harlean Carpentier

Quiz #12

TRUE OR FALSE

(Answers on page 105)

1. Peter Sellers starred in the movie *Dr. Strangelove.*

2. Jean Hersholt played Dr. Christian on the radio.

3. The star of the movie *Young Tom Edison* was Freddie Bartholomew.

4. Ava Gardner was born in South Carolina.

5. The movie *Rocky* starred and was written by Sylvester Stallone.

6. Hoot Gibson's real first name was Harold.

7. *The King and I* won the Oscar for Best Movie.

8. Marlow Brando's Broadway debut was in *I Remember Mama.*

9. Dorothy Malone began dancing at the age of three.

10. Tommy Dorsey gave Frank Sinatra his first job singing with a name band.

Roy Rogers and Gene Autry

Quiz #13

GENERAL QUESTIONS

(Answers on page 105)

1. Director Ron Howard's acting career really took off on what well-known television show?

2. Who starred in *The Fuller Brush Man?*

3. Who starred in *The Fuller Brush Girl?*

4. Name the studio the produced the *Our Gang* shorts.

5. How many times was Cary Grant married?

6. Who was the voice of *Frances, the Talking Mule?*

7. What famous comedian starred in *Oh, God?*

8. Audrey Hepburn played a princess in what movie?

9. Name the only movie that Marlow Brando directed.

10. Who said "Come with me to the Casbah?"

Quiz #14

FILM BIOGRAPHIES

Match the movie with the star.

(Answers on page 105)

1. Hans Christian Anderson
2. The Great Caruso
3. *Night and Day* (Cole Porter)
4. *The Benny Goodman Story*
5. *I'll Cry Tomorrow* (Lillian Roth)
6. The Buster Keaton Story
7. *The Joker is Wild* (Joe E. Lewis)
8. The Eddie Cantor Story
9. *Coal Miner's Daughter* (Loretta Lynn)
10. *The Man of a Thousand Faces* (Lon Chaney)

a. Steve Allen
b. Frank Sinatra
c. Keefe Brasselle
d. Danny Kaye
e. Sissy Spacek
f. Mario Lanza
g. James Cagney
h. Cary Grant
i. Donald O'Connor
j. Susan Haywood

Quiz #15

ANIMALS IN THE MOVIES

(Answers on page 106)

1. What was the name of Dale Evans' horse?

2. What kind of an animal was Bambi?

3. Who was the most popular animal in silent movies?

4. Name the movie about a Dolphin.

5. Who was Sylvester the cat always chasing?

6. What kind of a dog was Lassie?

7. Name Tarzan's Chimpanzee.

8. Tony, the horse, belonged to what cowboy?

9. What kind of an animal was Harvey?

10. Walt Disney's movie elephant was named ___.

Clark Gable

Quiz #16

CLARK GABLE

(Answers on page 106)

1. What state was Clark Gable from?

2. Name the movie where Clark took off his shirt and showed his bare chest?

3. Who was his co-star in that movie?

4. Name the character he played in *Gone With the Wind*.

5. Clark studied what subject in a night class at the University of Akron?

6. He enlisted in what branch of the service in World War II?

7. Who was his co-star in *Mogambo?*

8. What was Gable's real first name?

9. Why did many actresses hate to kiss him?

10. Who was his co-star in *Mutiny On the Bounty?*

Quiz #17

MULTIPLE CHOICE
(Answers on page 106)

1. Who was once Miss Pittsburgh?
    a) Florence Henderson   b) Shirley Jones   c) Mitzi Gaynor

2. The movie *Hellzapoppin* starred what comedy team?
    a) Olsen and Johnson   b) Martin and Lewis
    c) The 3 Stooges

3. What did Fred MacMurray once do for a living?
    a) bartender   b) dance-band singer   c) soda jerk

4. Marilyn Monroe once married what baseball player?
    a) Ted Williams   b) Mickey Mantle   c) Joe DiMaggio

5. In the movie *PT 109*, Cliff Robertson played what U.S. President?
    a) Harry Truman   b) Richard Nixon   c) John Kennedy

6. Where in New York was Kirk Douglas born?
    a) Amsterdam   b) The Bronx   c) New Rochelle

7. John Wayne won the Oscar for what movie?
    a) *True Grit*   b) *The Alamo*   c) *Sands of Iwo Jima*

8. Who did not appear in the movie *12 Angry Men*?
    a) Henry Fonda   b) John Payne   c) Jack Klugman

9. Who once worked for Minsky's Burlesque as a song-and-dance man?
    a) Gene Kelly   b) Donald O'Connor   c) Dan Dailey

10. Angela Lansbury's first movie was ___.
    a) *The Court Jester*   b) *Gaslight*   c) *The Purple Mask*

Quiz #18

MATCH THE ROBERT

(Answers on page 107)

1. Robert Downey, Jr.
2. Robert Altman
3. Robert Preston
4. Robert Alda
5. Robert Benchley
6. Robert DeNiro
7. Robert Blake
8. Robert Mitchum
9. Robert Redford
10. Robert Taylor

a. Appeared in *The Way We Were*
b. Sleepy-eyed actor
c. Directed *Nashville* and *M*A*S*H*
d. Starred in the movie *Chaplin*
e. Appeared in *Our Gang* comedies
f. Played George Gershwin in *Rhapsody in Blue*
g. Starred in *The Music Man*
h. Won the Oscar for Best Actor in *Raging Bull*
i. MGM star for 25 years
j. Often appeared in movies as a humorist-bumbler

Penny arcade cards

Quiz #19

GENERAL QUESTIONS
(Answers on page 107)

1. Name the #1 comedy team of the 1930s.

2. Name the #1 comedy team of the 1940s.

3. Name the #1 comedy team of the 1950s.

4. Who was known as the "sweater girl?"

5. The movie *Sun Valley Serenade* starred Glen Miller. Who planed Glen's manager?

6. What actor has won the most Oscars for Best Supporting Actor?

7. Who was Caesar Bandella?

8. In the movie *Mary Poppins*, what two roles did Dick Van Dyke play?

9. Name the actress who was known for her peek-a-boo hairdo.

10. Who was the youngest person to win an acting Academy Award for Best Supporting Actress?

Bette Davis

Quiz #20

BETTE DAVIS
(Answers on page 107)

1. How many times was Bette Davis nominated for the Academy Award?

2. Name the two movies that she won the Academy Award for.

3. She was once married to which actor?

4. Who was her co-star in *What Ever Happened to Baby Jane?*

5. Bette's character caused a scandal when she wore a red gown at a society ball. Name the movie.

6. In real life, which actress did Bette hate the most?

7. She played Apple Annie in which movie?

8. Bette was once the president of what motion picture organization?

9. Who was her co-star in *Hush…Hush, Sweet Charlotte?*

10. Name the character she played in *All About Eve.*

Quiz #21

FAMOUS MOVIE QUOTES

Who said it, and name the movie.

(Answers on page 108)

1. "Frankly, my dear, I don't give a damn."

2. "Here's Johnny!!"

3. "I'll be back."

4. "All right, Mr. DeMille. I'm ready for my closeup."

5. "Listen to me, mister. You're my knight in shining armor. Don't you forget it."

6. "Play it, Sam. Play 'As Times Goes By'."

7. "Mama always said that life was like a box of chocolates. You never know what you're gonna get."

8. "Why don't you come up and see me sometime?"

9. "Who's on first?"

10. "Nyuk…nyuk…nyuk."

Quiz #22

LIFE STORIES
Match the Hollywood star with his/her autobiography

(Answers on page 108)

1. Sammy Davis, Jr.
2. Bing Crosby
3. Fred Astaire
4. Katherine Hepburn
5. John Huston
6. Edward G. Robinson
7. Oscar Levant
8. Mae West
9. Fred Allen
10. Hedy Lamar

a. *Steps in Time*
b. *Me, The Story of My Life*
c. *All My Yesterdays*
d. *The Memoirs of an Amnesiac*
e. *Yes, I Can*
f. *Goodness Had Nothing To Do With It*
g. *Call Me Lucky*
h. *Ecstasy and Me*
i. *King Rebel*
j. *Much Ado About Me*

Ingrid Bergman

Quiz #23

GENERAL QUESTIONS

(Answers on page 108)

1. Who was known as "The Man of a Thousand Faces??

2. In the movie *Annie Get Your Gun,* who did Betty Hutton replace?

3. Dooley Wilson played the piano in what movie?

4. Who played Loretta Lynn in *Coal Miner's Daughter?*

5. Name the first actor to appear on the cover of *Time* magazine.

6. What was the name of the dog in the *Our Gang* shorts?

7. Mario Lanza starred in what movie about a well-known opera star?

8. Name the movie based on the life of Jerome Kern.

9. What actress was known as "The Oomph Girl?"

10. Name the actor who starred in *Bull Durham* and *Field of Dreams.*

Gum cards

Quiz #24

MULTIPLE CHOICE

(Answers on page 109)

1. Broderick Crawford played what kind of a role in *All the King's Men?*
    a) a prince   b) a politician   c) a king

2. *The Horn Blows at Midnight* featured which comedian?
    a) Fred Allen   b) Bob Hope   c) Jack Benny

3. What is the theme song of the movie *Blackboard Jungle?*
    a) "Sh-Boom"   b) "Rock Around the Clock"
    c) "Blueberry Hill"

4. William Holden's real last name is . . . .
    a) Breedle   b) Williams   c) Holderman

5. What instrument did Julia Roberts play in her high school band?
    a) clarinet   b) trumpet   c) trombone

6. Burt Lancaster's first movie was . . . .
    a) *Apache*   b) *All My Sons*   c) *The Killers*

7. Butterfly McQueen's real first name is . . . .
    a) Thelma   b) Constance   c) Beverly

8. In the movie *The Lost Weekend*, what was Ray Milland's addiction?
    a) a car thief   b) an alcoholic   c) a drug addict

9. Who gave John Wayne his first job in the movies?
    a) Will Rogers   b) Tom Mix   c) Buck Jones

10. What role did Orson Welles have in *Citizen Kane?*
    a) the writer   b) the director   c) the star

Quiz #25

NICKNAMES

Many movie personalities have nicknames. Name the nicknames.
(Answers on page 109)

1. John Wayne

2. Sylvester Stallone

3. Elizabeth Taylor

4. Jimmy Durante

5. Robert Wagner

6. Katherine Hepburn

7. Jerry "Curly" Howard

8. David Wark Griffith

9. Michael Sennett

10. Montgomery Clift

Quiz #26

GENERAL QUESTIONS

(Answers on page 109)

1. Actor Rock Hudson received his only Academy Award nomination for what movie?

2. What was the only X-rated movie to win the Academy Award for Best Movie?

3. Who replaced Donald O'Connor in the Francis movies?

4. What actor has been nominated the most times for the Academy Award?

5. Name the Laurel and Hardy movie that won the Academy Award for Best Short.

6. Who was known as The Oomph Girl?

7. What is Bud Abbott's real first name?

8. What was Grace Kelly's last movie?

9. What country has won the most Oscars for Best Foreign Language Film?

10. Who was the oldest person to win the Academy Award for Best Actress?

Marilyn Monroe

Quiz #27

MARILYN MONROE

(Answers on page 110)

1. What was Marilyn's last movie?

2. Who was her co-star?

3. Name the famous baseball player she was once married to.

4. How old was Marilyn when she died?

5. Name the movie where her dress flies up as she's standing on a subway grate.

6. Walt Disney said he created what character after Marilyn Monroe?

7. Who were her two co-stars in the movie *Some Like it Hot?*

8. What song did she sing for President Kennedy on national television?

9. Marilyn sang "Diamonds Are a Girl's Best Friend" in what movie?

10. Who did she telephone before she died?

Ginger Rogers

Quiz #28

OSCAR – TONY

Nine performers have won both the Oscar and the Tony, playing the same character. Match the performer with the movie/show:

(Answers on page 110)

1. Joel Grey
2. Yul Brynner
3. Anne Bancroft
4. Paul Scofield
5. Shirley Booth
6. Rex Harrison
7. Jose Ferrer
8. Jack Albertson
9. Lila Kedrova

a. *My Fair Lady*
b. *Zorba The Greek*
c. *Cabaret*
d. *The Subject Was Roses*
e. *The King and I*
f. *Cyrano de Bergerac*
g. *Come Back, Little Sheba*
h. *The Miracle Worker*
i. *A Man For All Seasons*

Quiz #29

TRUE OR FALSE

(Answers on page 110)

1. Stewart Granger's real name is Jimmy Stewart.

2. Albert Brooks' father was comedian Harry Einstein.

3. In the movie *Popeye*, Olive Oyl was played by Mia Farrow.

4. James Earl Jones was born in Texas.

5. In the movie *Some Like It Hot*, Tony Curtis does an imitation of Cary Grant.

6. Stacey Keach played detective Boston Blackie on television.

7. Katherine Hepburn and Audrey Hepburn are cousins.

8. W. C. Fields began his career as a juggler.

9. Eva Marie Saint starred in the movie *On the Waterfront*.

10. Abbott and Costello met in vaudeville.

Quiz #30

MULTIPLE CHOICE
(Answers on page 111)

1. The movie *Houdini* starred . . . .
   a) Tony Curtis   b) James Dean   c) James Coburn

2. Who was not a character in *The Little Rascals*?
   a) Alfalfa   b) Buckwheat   c) Shorty

3. Abbott and Costello's first movie was . . . .
   a) *Buck Privates*   b) *The Comedians*
   c) *The Gang's All Here*

4. Name the actress who starred in *Breakfast at Tiffany's*.
   a) Anne Archer   b) Audrey Hepburn   c) Estelle Parsons

5. Actor Neil Hamilton played what role on TV's *Batman*?
   a) The Joker   b) Alfred the Butler   c) The Penguin

6. What was the original name of *The Bowery Boys*?
   a) *The Teenagers*   b) *The Fun Hoodlums*
   c) *The Dead End Kids*

7. Who was the first western star?
   a) William S. Hart   b) Tom Mix   c) Hoot Gibson

8. Name the character Carl Weathers played in *Rocky*.
   a) Paulie   b) Spider Ricco   c) Apollo Creed

9. Elvis Presley starred in the movie . . . .
   a) *Kid Gavilan*   b) *Kid K.O.*   c) *Kid Galahad*

10. In the movie *Funny Girl*, name the character that Omar Sharif played.
    a) Nicky Arnstein   b) Billy Rose   c) Bobby Driscoll

Frank Sinatra

Quiz #31

FAMOUS MOVIE QUOTES

Who said it, and name the movie.

(Answers on page 111)

1. "I'm going to make him an offer he can't refuse."

2. "You know how to whistle, don't you, Steve? You just put your lips together and blow."

3. "Elementary, my dear Watson."

4. "Hello, gorgeous."

5. "Wait a minute. Wait a minute. You ain't heard nothin' yet."

6. "You can't handle the truth."

7. "Toto, I've got a feeling we're not in Kansas anymore."

8. "Made it, Ma. Top of the world."

9. "One morning I shot an elephant in my pajamas. How he got in my pajamas, I don't know!"

10. "Hasta la vista, baby."

Quiz #32

SPOUSES

Match the husbands and wives.

(Answers on page 111)

1. Phil Harris
2. Michael Douglas
3. Mel Ferrer
4. Richard Burton
5. Desi Arnaz
6. Jack Cassidy
7. Sylvester Stallone
8. Ronald Coleman
9. Paul Newman
10. Fred MacMurray

a. June Haver
b. Joanne Woodward
c. Benita Hume
d. Brigitte Nielson
e. Shirley Jones
f. Lucille Ball
g. Elizabeth Taylor
h. Audrey Hepburn
i. Catherine Zeta Jones
j. Alice Faye

Quiz #33

SILENT MOVIES

(Answers on page 112)

1. In *The Gold Rush*, what did Charlie Chaplin eat?

2. What was Laurel and Hardy's first film together?

3. Who were the silly policeman?

4. Name the comedian who was cross-eyed.

5. What were the first names of the three Talmadge Sisters.

6. Where was Ramon Nevarro born?

7. Who was known as "The Vamp?"

8. *The Mark of Zorro* starred what silent screen hero?

9. Who was the most famous director in the silent movie era?

10. *The General* starred what famous comedian?

Katherine Hepburn

Quiz #34

KATHERINE HEPBURN

(Answers on page 112)

1. Katherine was born and lived most of her life in what state?

2. She grew up loving western movies. Who was her screen idol?

3. Who was her significant other, even though they never married?

4. How many films did they make together?

5. Name her two co-stars in *The Philadelphia Story.*

6. What were her two hobbies?

7. How many Oscars did she win?

8. How many Golden Globes did she win?

9. She won the Tony Award for what Broadway musical?

10. Name the actor who played her son in *The Lion in Winter.*

Gum cards

Quiz #35

GENERAL QUESTIONS

(Answers on page 112)

1. What is Esther Williams best known for?

2. Who starred in the movie *The Invisible Man*?

3. Doris Day received one Academy Award nomination. Name the movie.

4. In the movie *It's a Wonderful Life*, what was the name of Jimmy Stewart's character?

5. James Cagney was the star of *Yankee Doodle Dandy*. Who played his sister?

6. Name the actress who played *Lolita*.

7. Who wrote the music for *The Sting*?

8. Who played the music for *The Sting*?

9. Jack Benny's bandleader on his radio show was who?

10. Name the first African-American to win an Academy Award.

Quiz #36

REAL NAMES

Match the actress with her real name.

(Answers on page 113)

1. Shelly Winters
2. Barbara Stanwyck
3. Marilyn Monroe
4. Natalie Wood
5. Lauren Bacall
6. Julie Andrews
7. Dorothy Lamour
8. Mary Pickford
9. Angie Dickinson
10. Lee Grant

a. Ruby Stevens
b. Julie Welles
c. Betty Jean Perske
d. Angeline Brown
e. Lyova Rosenthal
f. Shirley Schrift
g. Gladys Smith
h. Dorothy Kaumeyer
i. Norma Jean Mortenson
j. Natasha Gurdin

Quiz #37

GENERAL QUESTIONS

(Answers on page 113)

1. Name the two most famous dogs in the movies.

2. What is Bing Crosby's real name?

3. Who is Olivia de Havilland's well-known sister?

4. Name the short actor who had to stand on a box when he did close-ups with his leading lady?

5. Kevin Costner won the Oscar for best director for which movie?

6. Who was known for doing "The Tie Twiddle?"

7. Name the first Rambo movie.

8. Actor Robert Stack starred in what crime-fighting television series?

9. How old was James Dean when he died?

10. Who is Anjelica Huston's father?

Quiz #38

MATCH THE SONG WITH THE MOVIE
(Answers on page 113)

1.   "Zip-a-Dee-Doo-Dah"
2.   "Thank Heaven For Little Girls"
3.   "The Continental"
4.   "Under the Sea"
5.   "Up Where We Belong"
6.   "The Shadow Of Your Smile"
7.   "The Morning After"
8.   "The Man That Got Away"
9.   "A Spoonful of Sugar"
10. "The Boy Next Door"

a.   *The Little Mermaid*
b.   *The Sandpiper*
c.   *Song of the South*
d.   *Mary Poppins*
e.   *Gigi*
f.   *A Star Is Born*
g.   *An Officer And a Gentleman*
h.   *Meet Me In St. Louis*
i.   *The Gay Divorcee*
j.   *The Poseidon Adventure*

Quiz #39

HOLLYWOOD GOSSIP COLUMNISTS

Was it Louella Parsons, Jimmie Fidler, or Hedda Hopper

(Answers on page 114)

1. Who opened their radio show saying, "Good evening from Hollywood?"

2. Who concluded their radio show saying, "Good night to you, and I do mean you!"

3. Who began their career as a dancer on Broadway?

4. Who was known for wearing outrageous hats?

5. Who was a mystery guest three times on the CBS-TV show *What's My Line?*

6. Who once worked as a publicist for Cecil B. DeMille?

7. Who had a son that once played investigator Paul Drake on *The Perry Mason* TV series?

8. Who was a political ally of FBI director J. Edgar Hoover?

9. Who was the editor of *The Hollywood News?*

10. Who had a syndicated gossip column that was read by 20 million people?

Jack Nicholson

Quiz #40

JACK NICHOLSON

(Answers on page 114)

1. How many times has Jack Nicholson been nominated for the Oscar?

2. Jack often appears at what sports event?

3. He played Wilbur Force in what movie?

4. What role did he play in *Batman*?

5. Jack had a seventeen-year relationship with what actress?

6. Name his three female co-stars in *The Witches of Eastwick*.

7. In what movie did he say "Here's Johnny?"

8. He played Colonel Nathan Jessup in what film?

9. Who was his co-star in *The Bucket List*?

10. Name the movie for which he earned a Golden Globe nomination and was nominated for the Razzie Award?

Quiz #41

SONG WRITERS

Match the composer with the lyricist

(Answers on page 114)

1. Richard Rogers
2. George Gershwin
3. Irving Berlin
4. Jule Stein
5. Henry Mancini
6. Frederick Lowe
7. Sammy Fain
8. Burt Bacharach
9. John Kander
10. Harold Arlen

a. Sammy Cahn
b. Hal David
c. Johnny Mercer
d. Paul Francis Webster
e. Ira Gershwin
f. Fred Ebb
g. Oscar Hammerstein II
h. E. Y. Harburg
i. Alan Jay Lerner
j. Irving Berlin

Quiz #42

TRUE OR FALSE

(Answers on page 115)

1. Mickey Rooney replaced Donald O'Connor in the seventh *Francis* movie.

2. The movie *Houseboat* starred Sophia Loren.

3. Fred Astaire danced in *An American in Paris*.

4. "Gonna Fly Now" was the theme song of *Dr. No*.

5. The voice of Mr. Boynton on radio's *Our Miss Brooks* was played by Jeff Chandler.

6. In the movie *The Helen Morgan Story*, Ann Blyth's singing was dubbed by Doris Day.

7. The song "Thumbelina" came from the movie *Hans Christian Anderson*.

8. Margaret O'Brien was the first Tammy.

9. Lana Turner starred in *The Postman Always Rings Twice*.

10. In the movie *Going My Way*, the song "Swinging On a Star" was sung by Dick Haymes.

The Marx Brothers

Quiz #43

THE MARX BROTHERS

(Answers on page 115)

1. Name the five Marx Brothers.

2. They had a well-known stage door mother. What was her first name?

3. The brothers were cousins to what radio personalities?

4. What was their first musical comedy on Broadway?

5. Groucho played what musical instrument?

6. Which brother's real name was Herbert?

7. Name Groucho's famous radio/TV show.

8. Who was his announcer?

9. The brothers made movies for three different motion picture companies. Name them.

10. In 1977, what great honor did the Marx Brothers receive?

Penny arcade cards

Quiz #44

GENERAL QUESTIONS

(Answers on page 115)

1. Name the lady who was known as "The Brazilian Bombshell.

2. Who produced the movie *Around the World in 80 Days?*

3. What was the last movie that James Cagney appeared in?

4. The first person to play Superman in the movies was who?

5. Where was Greta Garbo born?

6. Name the horse that was known as "The Wonder Horse?"

7. Who was the first Tarzan?

8. Quasimodo was a character in what movie?

9. Robert Young starred in what radio and television series?

10. In what city does *The Sting* take place?

Quiz #45

MULTIPLE CHOICE
(Answers on page 116)

1. Tarzan's chimpanzee was named . . . .
   a) Cheetah   b) Muggs   c) Bonzo

2. In *The Public Enemy*, James Cagney pushes a grapefruit in whose face?
   a) Mae Bush   b) Mae Clark   c) Mae Young

3. Name the movie in which Fred Astaire dances on the ceiling.
   a) *Royal Wedding*   b) *Top Hat*   c) *Easter Parade*

4. Dean Martin and Jerry Lewis' first movie was . . . .
   a) *The Caddy*   b) *The Bellboy*   c) *My Friend Irma*

5. What was Shirley Jones' occupation in *The Music Man*?
   a) School teacher   b) Librarian   c) Secretary

6. Who played Sally Bowles in *Cabaret*?
   a) Judy Garland   b) Liza Minnelli   c) Debbie Reynolds

7. In the movie *Miracle on 34th Street*, who played Santa Claus?
   a) Edmund Gwen   b) Wayne Morris   c) Robert Young

8. What was Henry Fonda's last movie?
   a) *Fort Apache*   b) *In Harm's Way*   c) *On Golden Pond*

9. Who played the Scarecrow in *The Wiz*?
   a) Michael Jackson   b) Ray Bolger   c) Bill Cosby

10. Don Ameche played what famous inventor?
    a) Thomas Edison   b) Marconi
    c) Alexander Graham Bell

Quiz #46

MATCH THE WILLIAM

(Answers on page 116)

1. William Bendix
2. William Holden
3. William Powell
4. William Boyd
5. William Hurt
6. William Hickey
7. William Friedkin
8. William Gargan
9. William Wellman
10. William Wyler

a. Starred in a series of *Thin Man* films
b. Directed *The High and The Mighty*
c. Won the Academy Award for Best Actor in *Stalag 17*
d. Played detective Martin Kane on radio and television
e. Directed *The Exorcist* and *The French Connection*
f. Starred in *The Life of Riley* on radio and television
g. Played Hopalong Cassidy
h. Won the Academy Award for Best Supporting Actor in *Prizzi's Honor*
i. Won the Academy Award for Best Actor in *Kiss of the Spider Woman*
j. Won the Academy Award for Best Director for *Ben-Hur*

Quiz #47

GENERAL QUESTIONS

(Answers on page 116)

1. Who was known as "The Queen of the West?"

2. What do Warner Oland and Sidney Toler have in common?

3. Actor Dwayne Johnson was once a pro wrestler. What name did he use?

4. Who is the only person named Oscar to win an Oscar?

5. In the movie *Cabaret,* what was the name of the nightclub?

6. What was the first 3-D movie?

7. Name the first talking movie.

8. What year did it come out?

9. Who wrote *Gone With the Wind?*

10. Name the comedian who was the master of the slow burn.

Quiz #48

FILM DIRECTORS

Match the movie with the director.

(Answers on page 117)

1. *Schindler's List*
2. *Annie Hall*
3. *Gigi*
4. *Some Like It Hot*
5. *Guess Who's Coming To Dinner*
6. *Midnight Cowboy*
7. *Goodfellas*
8. *Fiddler On The Roof*
9. *Treasure of Sierra Madre*
10. *On the Waterfront*

a. Martin Scorsese
b. Elia Kazan
c. Stephen Spielberg
d. Billy Wilder
e. Woody Allen
f. John Huston
g. Norman Jewison
h. Stanley Kramer
i. Vincente Minnelli
j. John Schlesinger

The Three Stooges

Quiz #49

THE THREE STOOGES

(Answers on page 117)

1. How many comedians were in the stooges?

2. Name them.

3. The Three Stooges made all of their shorts for what motion picture company?

4. How many shorts did they make?

5. Which stooge had the nickname "Babe?"

6. Name the stooge who played the big bass.

7. How many feature films did they make?

8. What was the name of their first feature film?

9. Which stooge came from Philadelphia?

10. Name the stooge who appeared with W. C. Fields in *The Bank Dick*.

Quiz #50

FAMOUS MOVIE QUOTES

Who said it, and name the movie.

(Answers on page 117)

11. "Fasten your seatbelts. It's going to be a bumpy night."

2. "Yo, Adrian."

3. "Today, I consider myself the luckiest man on the face of the earth."

4. "You don't understand. I coulda had class. I coulda been a contender."

5. "My mother thanks you. My father thanks you. My sister thanks you. And I thank you."

6. "Mrs. Robinson, you're trying to seduce me, aren't you?"

7. "Go ahead, make my day."

8. "Mother of mercy. Is this the end of Rico?"

9. "A martini. Shaken, not stirred."

10. "Well, here's another nice mess you've gotten me into."

Quiz #51

GENERAL QUESTIONS

(Answers on page 118)

1. What was Greta Garbo's most famous line?

2. Who was the leader of the Bowery Boys?

3. What actress once had her legs insured for 1 million dollars?

4. Who played detective Matt Helm?

5. George Raft began his show-biz career doing what?

6. In the 1930s, who was known as "The King of Hollywood?"

7. Who played Henry Aldrich in the movies?

8. Marjorie Main and Percy Killbride played what movie duo?

9. Who was known as "The King of Jazz?"

10. Who was Alan Alda's father?

Hoodsie covers

Quiz #52

SPOUSES

Match the husbands and wives.

(Answers on page 118)

1. Ronald Reagan
2. Orson Welles
3. Frank Sinatra
4. Blake Edwards
5. Clark Gable
6. Charles Bronson
7. Irving Thalberg
8. Eddie Fisher
9. Lex Barker
10. Carlo Ponti

a. Julie Andrews
b. Carole Lombard
c. Sophia Loren
d. Jane Wyman
e. Esther Williams
f. Ava Gardner
g. Norma Shearer
h. Jill Ireland
i. Debbie Reynolds
j. Rita Hayworth

Elizabeth Taylor

Quiz #53

ELIZABETH TAYLOR

(Answers on page 118)

1. Elizabeth Taylor won her first Oscar for what movie?

2. She won her second Oscar for what movie?

3. What is the color of Elizabeth's eyes?

4. Where was she born?

5. Name her first husband?

6. How old was Elizabeth when she made *Lassie Come Home*?

7. Name the singer who left Debbie Reynolds to marry her.

8. In 1963, Elizabeth received one million dollars to star in what movie?

9. She made her Broadway debut in which play?

10. Name her co-star in *The Sandpiper* and *The Taming of the Shrew*.

Quiz #54

MATCH THE SONG WITH THE MOVIE

(Answers on page 119)

1. "The Windmills Of Your Mind"
2. "You Take My Breath Away"
3. "Supercalifragilisticexpialidocious"
4. "Raindrops Keep Fallin' On My Head"
5. "Too-Ra-Loo-Ra-Loo-Ra"
6. "We May Never Love Like This Again"
7. "I Just Called To Say I Love You"
8. "Sweet Leilani"
9. "The Night They Invented Champagne"
10. "A Very Precious Love"

a. Marjorie Morningstar
b. *Gigi*
c. *Waikiki Wedding*
d. *The Woman In Red*
e. *The Towering Inferno*
f. *Butch Cassidy and the Sundance Kid*
g. *Going My Way*
h. *Mary Poppins*
i. *Top Gun*
j. *The Thomas Crown Affair*

Quiz #55

NICKNAMES

Many movie personalities have nicknames. Name the nicknames.

(Answers on page 119)

1. Humphrey Bogart
2. Lauren Bacall
3. Hopalong Cassidy
4. Milton Berle
5. Doris Day
6. Cecil B. DeMille
7. Oliver Hardy
8. Don Barry
9. Angelina Jolie
10. George Hayes

Quiz #56

MULTIIPLE CHOICE

(Answers on page 119)

1. In the movie *Written On the Wind*, name the vocal group that sang the opening theme.
    a) The Four Lads   b) The Four Aces   c) The Four Preps

2. Betty Hutton replaced what actress in *The Greatest Show on Earth*?
    a) Shirley Temple   b) Margaret O'Brien   c) Judy Garland

3. In 1970 Frank Sinatra presented a special Academy Award to what actor?
    a) Cary Grant   b) James Cagney   c) Charlie Chaplin

4. Jerry Lewis played seven different roles in what film?
    a) *The Bellboy*   b) *The Family Jewels*   c) *The Caddy*

5. Herman Wouk wrote what famous movie?
    a) *The Caine Mutiny*   b) *Mogambo*   c) *Little Big Man*

6. Mel Blanc was the voice of what cartoon character?
    a) Bugs Bunny   b) Tweety Bird   c) Sylvester the Cat

7. Mario Lanza starred and sang in what movie?
    a) *Paint Your Wagon*   b) *The Student Prince*   c) *The King and I*

8. As a child, Milton Berle appeared in a movie with what great comedian?
    a) Stan Laurel   b) Charlie Chase   c) Charlie Chaplin

9. Where was Gene Hackman born?
    a) California   b) New York   c) New Jersey

10. Morgan Freeman appeared in what show on Broadway?
    a) *Hello, Dolly!*   b) *Purlie*   c) *The Wiz*

Quiz #57

LIFE STORIES

Match the Hollywood star with his/her autobiography:

(Answers on page 120)

1. Ethel Merman
2. Mickey Rooney
3. Buster Keaton
4. Larry Fine
5. Pat O'Brien
6. Hedda Hopper
7. Maurice Chevalier
8. Dorothy Lamour
9. Eddie Cantor
10. Lawrence Olivier

a. *Life is Too Short*
b. *The Wind At My Back*
c. *Confessions Of An Actor*
d. *With Love*
e. *My Side of the Road*
f. *Stroke of Luck*
g. *My Life Is In Your Hands*
h. *Who Could Ask For Anything More*
i. *My Wonderful World of Slapstick*
j. *The Whole Truth and Nothing But*

Sean Connery as James Bond

Quiz #58

BOND...JAMES BOND

(Answers on page 120)

1. Who created James Bond?

2. What was the first Bond movie?

3. Who was his love interest in that movie?

4. Name the actor who starred in the most James Bond films.

5. How many Bond movies have been made?

6. Name the tallest actor who played James Bond.

7. Name the shortest actor who played James Bond.

8. What character did Richard Kiel play in two Bond movies?

9. How did James Bond like his martinis?

10. Who wrote his autobiography, *My Word Is My Bond*?

Quiz #59

TRUE OR FALSE

(Answers on page 120)

1. Gene Kelly directed the movie *Hello, Dolly*.

2. In *Casablanca*, Humphrey Bogart was the owner of Rick's Café.

3. Ginger Rogers won her Oscar for *Mrs. Minever*.

4. Claude Rains starred in *The Invisible Man*.

5. Ava Gardner was known as "The Sweater Girl."

6. Paul Newman was color blind.

7. *Citizen Cane* was loosely based on the life of Harry Truman.

8. The movie *The Joker Is Wild* was the life story of Joe E. Brown.

9. Frank Sinatra sang on radio's *Your Hit Parade*.

10. Doris Day received her only Academy Award nomination for *Calamity Jane*.

Quiz #60

MATCH THE JOHN

(Answers on page 121)

1. John Wayne
2. John Barrymore
3. John Huston
4. John Lithgow
5. John Mills
6. John Payne
7. John Cassavetes
8. John Gielgud
9. John Williams
10. John Schlesinger

a. Won the Academy Award as Best Director for *Midnight Cowboy*
b. Emmy and Tony Award winner
c. Known as "The Great Profile"
d. Won the Academy Award as Best Supporting Actor in *Arthur*
e. Nominated for Best Supporting Actor in *The Dirty Dozen*
f. Directed *Prizzi's Honor*
g. Known for appearing in musicals in the 1940s and westerns in the 1950s
h. Made more movies than any other movie star
i. Multi Academy Award winner as a composer
j. Won the Academy Award as Best Supporting Actor in *Ryan's Daughter*

Jennifer Jones

Quiz #61

TRUE OR FALSE

(Answers on page 121)

1. Bette Davis' real first name is Ruth.

2. Judy Garland was 14 when she made *The Wizard of Oz*.

3. W. C. Fields' last starring role was in *The Bank Dick*.

4. Minnesota Fats played himself in *The Hustler*.

5. *I'll See You In My Dreams* was the life story of Cole Porter.

6. Janet Leigh and Vivian Leigh were sisters.

7. Dean Martin played Matt Helm in several movies.

8. Ava Gardner's middle name is Lavinia.

9. *Rosebud* was a boat.

10. Peter Sellers played Inspector Clouseau.

Quiz #62

REAL NAMES

Match the actor with his real name.

(Answers on page 121)

1. Kirk Douglas
2. Alan Alda
3. George Burns
4. John Wayne
5. Gene Wilder
6. W. C. Fields
7. Rodney Dangerfield
8. Red Buttons
9. Rochester
10. Danny Thomas

a. Marion Morrison
b. Eddie Anderson
c. Issur Danielovitch
d. Gerald Silberman
e. Amos Jacobs
f. Aaron Chwatt
g. Alphonso D'Abruzzo
h. Nathan Birnbaum
i. William Claude Dukenfield
j. Jacob Cohen

Quiz #63

GENERAL QUESTIONS

(Answers on page 122)

1. Name the camp in the movie *Friday, the Thirteenth*.

2. What was Rocky's last name?

3. Mike Todd was best known for producing what movie?

4. How many Matt Helm movies have there been?

5. In the movie *The Wiz*, who played Dorothy?

6. What was Annette Funicello and Frankie Avalon's first movie together?

7. In the movie *The Natural*, what was the name of the baseball team that Robert Redford played for?

8. Name the first *Dirty Harry* movie.

9. Who played Abraham Lincoln in two movies?

10. Who is Samuel Goldfish?

Walt Disney

Quiz #64

WALT DISNEY

(Answers on page 122)

1. What was the first Disney animated feature?

2. What was the second Disney animated feature?

3. Name the Disney character who was introduced in 1934.

4. Disneyland Park in California opened in what year?

5. Name the first Walt Disney cartoon.

6. Who was the host of television's *Mickey Mouse Club*?

7. What was Mickey Mouse's original name?

8. Name the Seven Dwarfs.

9. Who was Adriana Caselotti?

10. Name the first Disney live-action film?

Quiz #65

REAL NAMES

Match the actor with his real name.

(Answers on page 122)

1. Danny Kaye
2. Boris Karloff
3. John Garfield
4. Mickey Rooney
5. Jack Benny
6. Rex Harrison
7. Jeff Chandler
8. Fred Allen
9. Woody Allen
10. Michael Caine

a. Benny Kubelski
b. John Florence Sullivan
c. David Kominsky
d. Joe Yule, Jr.
e. Maurice Micklewhite
f. Allen Stewart Konigsberg
g. William Henry Pratt
h. Julius Garfinkle
i. Ira Grossell
j. Reginald Carey

Quiz #66

FAMOUS MOVIE QUOTES

Who said it, and name the movie.

(Answers on page 123)

1. "Stella! Hey, Stella!"

2. "Rosebud."

3. "You talking to me?"

4. "The pallet with the poison's in the vessel with the pestle. The chalice from the palace had the brew that is true!"

5. "I'll get you, my pretty, and your little dog, too."

6. "No wire hangers, ever."

7. "It was Beauty that killed the beast."

8. "Shane. Shane. Come back!"

9. "I love you, Spartacus."

10. "A boy's best friend is his mother."

Betty Grable

Quiz #67

MULTIPLE CHOICE

(Answers on page 123)

1. What was the name of Lone Ranger's horse?
   a) Trigger b) Champion c) Silver

2. Who does not appear in Singin' In The Rain?
   a) Debbie Reynolds b) Gene Kelly c) Ray Bolger

3. Michael Keaton once played what comic book character?
   a) Superman b) The Flash c) Batman

4. *What movie/TV personality used to sing* See The USA In Your Chevrolet?
   a) Patti Page b) Dinah Shore c) Edie Adams

5. *Who starred and directed* The Gator?
   a) Burt Reynolds b) Steven Segal c) Clint Eastwood

6. Doris Day co-starred with Gordon MacRae in what movie?
   a) *On Moonlight Bay* b) *Pajama Game*
   c) *Love Me Or Leave Me*

7. What actor once did a TV commercial for Canada Dry?
   a) Jack Webb b) Howard Duff c) Broderick Crawford

8. Name the radio and television show that Eva Arden starred in.
   a) *Our Miss Brooks* b) *A Date With Judy*
   c) *Meet Corliss Archer*

9. *The movie* The Five Pennies *starred who?*
   a) Danny Thomas b) Red Buttons c) Danny Kaye

10. Meryl Streep made her film debut in . . . .
    a) *Julia* b) *Postcards From The Edge*
    c) *Sophie's Choice*

Paul Newman

Quiz #68

PAUL NEWMAN

(Answers on page 123)

1. Where did Paul Newman make his home?

2. What branch of the service was he in?

3. Name the movie that won Paul the Academy Award for Best Actor.

4. He co-starred with Elizabeth Taylor in what movie?

5. What sport did Paul partake in?

6. Name the camp that Paul started for seriously ill children.

7. Paul played an alcoholic attorney in what movie?

8. What kind of a car did he drive in *Hud*?

9. Paul co-starred with Robert Redford in what two movies?

10. Name the movie that was based on hockey.

Quiz #69

FILM BIOGRAPHIES

Match the movie with the star.

(Answers on page 124)

1. *The Jolson Story*
2. *W. C. Fields and Me*
3. *The Glen Miller Story*
4. *Yankee Doodle Dandy* (George M. Cohan)
5. *The George Raft Story*
6. *Swanee River* (Stephen Foster)
7. *With a Song in My Heart* (Jane Froman)
8. *The Gene Krupa Story*
9. *Stars and Stripes Forever* (John Philip Sousa)
10. *Rhapsody In Blue* (George Gershwin)

a. James Cagney
b. Susan Hayward
c. Don Ameche
d. Larry Parks
e. Robert Alda
f. Rod Steiger
g. Clifton Webb
h. James Stewart
i. Sal Mineo
j. Ray Danton

Quiz #70

GENERAL QUESTIONS

(Answers on page 124)

1. Bing Crosby and Grace Kelly made two movies together. Name them.

2. What do Paul McCarthy and Charlie Chaplin have in common?

3. In the movie *Singin' in the Rain*, what was the name of the movie studio?

4. Who played Hannibal Lecter in *Silence of the Lambs*?

5. How do all the MGM movies begin?

6. What was Dirty Harry's last name?

7. Chester Morris played what detective?

8. Name the movie star that once had her legs insured for one million dollars.

9. Who wrote the theme song for the movie *Shaft*?

10. What was Orson Welles' most famous movie?

Jack Lemmon

Quiz #71

JACK LEMMON

(Answers on page 124)

1. What college did Jack Lemmon attend?

2. Jack won the Oscar for Best Actor in what movie?

3. Jack won the Oscar for Best Supporting Actor in what movie?

4. How many times was he nominated for the Academy Award?

5. Who was Jack's co-star in *The Odd Couple*?

6. He played an alcoholic in what movie?

7. Who was Jack's first mate in *The Wackiest Ship in the Army*?

8. Jack won an Emmy for what TV movie?

9. Name the only movie that Jack Lemmon directed.

10. He played a businessman in what movie?

Penny arcade cards

Quiz #72

SPOUSES

Match the husbands and wives.

(Answers on page 125)

1. Cary Grant
2. Al Jolson
3. Charlie Chaplin
4. Dick Powell
5. Steven Spielberg
6. Humphrey Bogart
7. Billy Bob Thornton
8. Vincente Minnelli
9. Tony Martin
10. Robert Taylor

a. Amy Irving
b. Lauren Bacall
c. Ruby Keeler
d. Barbara Stanwyck
e. Angelina Jolie
f. Cyd Charisse
g. Dyan Cannon
h. Paulette Goddard
i. Judy Garland
j. June Allyson

ANSWERS

Quiz #1 *(from page 1)*

1. The Jets and the Sharks
2. Isaac Hayes
3. Bonnie Parker and Clyde Barrow
4. *This Is Cinerama*
5. Henry
6. Gandhi
7. Theda Bara
8. Daisy
9. Titanic
10. Willie Stark

Quiz #2 *(from page 3)*

1. Lauren Bacall
2. The Navy
3. *The African Queen*
4. Audrey Hepburn
5. Philip Marlowe
6. *The Harder They Fall*
7. Primo Carnera
8. *Angels With Dirty Faces*
9. John Huston
10. The Rat Pack (When Bogie died, Frank Sinatra replaced him.)

Quiz #3 *(from page 4)*

1. c
2. b
3. b
4. a & b
5. a
6. a
7. c
8. a
9. b
10. c

Quiz #4 *(from page 5)*

1. Sylvester
2. Bluto
3. Andy
4. Little Lulu
5. Don Knotts
6. Huey, Dewey, and Louie
7. A cat
8. William Hanna and Joe Barbera
9. Minnie Mouse
10. Carrots

Quiz #5 *(from page 7)*

1. f
2. h
3. d
4. j
5. a
6. i
7. b
8. c
9. g
10. e

Quiz #6 *(from page 8)*

1. *Holiday Inn* and *White Christmas*
2. Barry Fitzgerald
3. James Stewart
4. Jean Shepherd
5. Natalie Wood
6. *The Lemon Drop Kid*
7. Jim Carrey
8. *Going My Way*
9. *Mame*
10. Jimmy Durante

Quiz #7 *(from page 9)*

1. b
2. e
3. i
4. a
5. h
6. c
7. f
8. d
9. g
10. j

Quiz #8 *(from page 10)*

1. Walter Brennan (won three times)
2. Shelly Winters
3. Suspense
4. Barbara Stanwyck
5. *The Killers* (1964)
6. Marilyn Monroe
7. Lou Gossett, Jr.
8. Dustin Hoffman and Jon Voight
9. *The Flying Nun*
10. Hoboken, New Jersey

Quiz #9 *(from page 11)*

1. e
2. d
3. g
4. b
5. h
6. a
7. c
8. f
9. j
10. i

Quiz #10 *(from page 13)*

1. *Psycho*
2. *Rebecca* (1940)
3. Hitch
4. *Rear Window*
5. *Whatever Will Be, Will Be*
6. Gregory Peck and Ingrid Bergman
7. The Irving Thalberg Memorial Award
8. *Dial M For Murder, Rear Window,* and *To Catch a Thief*
9. *Alfred Hitchcock Presents*
10. *Suspicion*

Quiz #11 *(from page 14)*

1. g
2. d
3. j
4. c
5. f
6. e
7. h
8. i
9. a
10. b

Quiz #12 *(from page 15)*

1. True
2. True
3. False (It was Mickey Rooney.)
4. False (She was born in North Carolina.)
5. True
6. False (His first name was Edmund.)
7. False
8. True
9. True
10. False (It was Harry James.)

Quiz #13 *(from page 17)*

1. *The Andy Griffith Show*
2. Red Skelton
3. Lucille Ball
4. Hall Roach Studio
5. Five times
6. Chill Wills
7. George Burns
8. *Roman Holiday*
9. *One-Eyed Jacks*
10. Charles Boyer

Quiz #14 *(from page 18)*

1. d
2. f
3. h
4. a
5. j
6. i
7. b
8. c
9. e
10. g

Quiz #15 *(from page 19)*

1. Buttermilk
2. A deer
3. Rin Tin Tin
4. *Flipper*
5. Tweety
6. A collie
7. Cheetah
8. Tom Mix
9. A Rabbit
10. Dumbo

Quiz #16 *(from page 21)*

1. Ohio
2. *It Happened One Night*
3. Claudette Colbert
4. Rhett Butler
5. Medicine
6. Army Air Corps
7. Ava Gardner
8. William
9. They claimed he had bad breath.
10. Charles Laughton

Quiz #17 *(from page 22)*

1. b
2. a
3. b
4. c
5. c
6. a
7. a
8. b
9. c
10. b

Quiz #18 *(from page 23)*

1. d
2. c
3. g
4. f
5. j
6. h
7. e
8. b
9. a
10. i

Quiz #19 *(from page 25)*

1. Laurel and Hardy
2. Abbott and Costello
3. Martin and Lewis
4. Lana Turner
5. Milton Berle
6. Walter Brennan (3 times)
7. Little Caesar's real name
8. Bert and Old Man Dawes
9. Veronica Lake
10. Tatum O'Neal (age 10 for *Paper Moon*)

Quiz #20 *(from page 27)*

1. Eleven times
2. *Dangerous* (1935) and *Jezebel* (1938)
3. Gary Merrill
4. Joan Crawford
5. *Jezebel*
6. Joan Crawford
7. *A Pocketful of Miracles*
8. The Academy of Motion Pictures Arts and Sciences
9. Olivia de Havilland
10. Margo Channing

Quiz #21 *(from page 28)*
1. Clark Gable – *Gone With the Wind*
2. Jack Nicholson – *The Shining*
3. Arnold Schwarzenegger – *The Terminator*
4. Gloria Swanson – *Sunset Boulevard*
5. Katharine Hepburn – *On Golden Pond*
6. Humphrey Bogart – *Casablanca*
7. Tom Hanks – *Forrest Gump*
8. Mae West – *She Done Him Wrong*
9. Bud Abbott – *The Naughty Nineties*
10. Curly Howard – many Three Stooges shorts

Quiz #22 *(from page 29)*
1. e
2. g
3. a
4. b
5. i
6. c
7. d
8. f
9. j
10. h

Quiz #23 *(from page 31)*
1. Lon Chaney
2. Judy Garland
3. Casablanca
4. Sissy Spacek
5. Charlie Chaplin
6. Pete
7. *The Great Caruso*
8. Jerome Kern
9. Ann Sheridan
10. Kevin Costner

Quiz #24 *(from page 33)*

1. b
2. c
3. b
4. a
5. a
6. c
7. a
8. b
9. b (moving the props)
10. a-b-c (He also was the producer.)

Quiz #25 *(from page 34)*

1. Duke
2. Sly
3. Liz
4. Schnozzola
5. R. J.
6. Katie
7. Babe
8. D. W.
9. Mack
10. Monty

Quiz #26 *(from page 35)*

1. *Giant*
2. *Midnight Cowboy*
3. Mickey Rooney
4. Jack Nicholson
5. *The Music Box* (1932)
6. Ann Sheridan
7. William
8. *High Society*
9. Italy
10. Jessica Tandy (age 81, for *Driving Miss Daisy*)

Quiz #27 *(from page 37)*
1. *The Misfits*
2. Clark Gable
3. Joe Dimaggio
4. Thirty-six
5. *The Seven Year Itch*
6. Tinkerbell (from *Peter Pan*)
7. Jack Lemmon and Tony Curtis
8. "Happy Birthday"
9. *Gentlemen Prefer Blondes*
10. Peter Lawford

Quiz #28 *(from page 39)*
1. c
2. e
3. h
4. i
5. g
6. a
7. f
8. d
9. b

Quiz #29 *(from page 40)*
1. True
2. True
3. False (She was played by Shelly Duvall.)
4. False (He was born in Mississippi.)
5. True
6. False (He played detective Mike Hammer.)
7. False
8. True
9. True
10. False (They met in Burlesque.)

Quiz #30 *(from page 41)*

1. a
2. c
3. a
4. b
5. b
6. c
7. a
8. c
9. c
10. a

Quiz #31 *(from page 43)*

1. Marlon Brando – *The Godfather*
2. Lauren Bacall – *To Have and Have Not*
3. Basil Rathbone – *The Adventures of Sherlock Holmes*
4. Barbra Streisand – *Funny Girl*
5. Al Jolson – *The Jazz Singer*
6. Jack Nicholson – *A Few Good Men*
7. Judy Garland – *The Wizard of Oz*
8. James Cagney – *White Heat*
9. Groucho Marx – *Animal Crackers*
10. Arnold Schwarzenegger – *Terminator 2: Judgment Day*

Quiz #32 *(from page 44)*

1. j
2. i
3. h
4. g
5. f
6. e
7. d
8. c
9. b
10. a

Quiz #33 *(from page 45)*

1. His shoe
2. *Putting the Pants on Philip*
3. The Keystone Cops
4. Ben Turpin
5. Norma, Natalie, and Constance
6. Mexico
7. Theda Bara
8. Douglas Fairbanks
9. D. W. Griffith
10. Buster Keaton

Quiz #34 *(from page 47)*

1. Connecticut
2. William S. Hart
3. Spencer Tracy
4. Nine films
5. Cary Grant and Jimmy Stewart
6. Painting and sculpturing
7. Four
8. Six
9. Coco
10. Anthony Hopkins

Quiz #35 *(from page 49)*

1. Swimming
2. Claude Rains
3. *Pillow Talk*
4. George Bailey
5. Jeanne Cagney (his real-life sister)
6. Sue Lyon
7. Scott Joplin
8. Marvin Hamlish
9. Phil Harris
10. Hattie McDaniel (Best Supporting Actress in 1939 for *Gone With the Wind*)

Quiz #36 *(from page 50)*

1. f
2. a
3. i
4. j
5. c
6. b
7. h
8. g
9. d
10. e

Quiz #37 *(from page 51)*

1. Lassie and Rin Tin Tin
2. Harry Lillis Crosby
3. Joan Fontaine
4. Alan Ladd
5. *Dances With Wolves*
6. Oliver Hardy
7. *First Blood*
8. *The Untouchables*
9. Twenty-four
10. John Huston

Quiz #38 *(from page 52)*

1. c
2. e
3. i
4. a
5. g
6. b
7. j
8. f
9. d
10. h

Quiz #39 *(from page 53)*
1. Louella Parsons
2. Jimmie Fidler
3. Hedda Hopper
4. Hedda Hopper
5. Louella Parsons
6. Jimmie Fidler
7. Hedda Hopper
8. Hedda Hopper
9. Jimmie Fidler
10. Louella Parsons

Quiz #40 *(from page 55)*
1. Twelve times (8 for Best Actor, 4 for Best Supporting Actor)
2. Pro basketball. He is an avid Los Angeles Lakers fan.
3. *The Little Shop of Horrors*
4. The Joker
5. Anjelica Huston
6. Cher, Michelle Pfeiffer, Susan Sarandon
7. *The Shining*
8. *A Few Good Men*
9. Morgan Freeman
10. *Hoffa*

Quiz #41 *(from page 56)*
1. g
2. e
3. j
4. a
5. c
6. i
7. d
8. b
9. f
10. h

Quiz #42 *(from page 57)*
1. True
2. True
3. False (It was Gene Kelly.)
4. False (It was the theme song of *Rocky*.)
5. True
6. False (The singer was Gogi Grant.)
7. True
8. False (The first Tammy was Debbie Reynolds.)
9. True
10. False (The singer was Bing Crosby.)

Quiz #43 *(from page 59)*
1. Groucho, Chico, Harpo, Zeppo, and Gummo
2. Minnie
3. Mary Livingston
4. *The Coconuts* (1929)
5. *The guitar*
6. Zeppo
7. *You Bet Your Life*
8. George Fenneman
9. Paramount, MGM, United Artists
10. They were inducted into the Motion Picture Hall of Fame.

Quiz #44 *(from page 61)*
1. Carmen Miranda
2. Mike Todd
3. Ragtime
4. Kirk Allen
5. Sweden
6. Champion
7. Elmo Lincoln
8. *The Hunchback of Notre Dame*
9. *Father Knows Beset*
10. Chicago

Quiz #45 *(from page 62)*

1. a
2. b
3. a
4. c
5. b
6. b
7. a
8. c
9. a
10. c

Quiz #46 *(from page 63)*

1. f
2. c
3. a
4. g
5. i
6. h
7. e
8. d
9. b
10. j

Quiz #47 *(from page 64)*

1. Dale Evans
2. They both played Charlie Chan.
3. The Rock
4. Oscar Hammerstein
5. The Kit Kat Club
6. Bwana Devil
7. *The Jazz Singer*
8. 1927
9. Margaret Mitchell
10. Edgar Kennedy

Quiz #48 *(from page 65)*
1. c
2. e
3. i
4. d
5. h
6. j
7. a
8. g
9. f
10. b

Quiz #49 *(from page 67)*
1. Six
2. Moe Howard, Curly Howard, Shemp Howard, Larry Fine, Joe Besser, Joe DeRita
3. Columbia Pictures
4. 196
5. Curly
6. Curly
7. Seven
8. *Have Rocket Will Travel*
9. Larry
10. Shemp

Quiz #50 *(from page 68)*
1. Bette Davis – *All About Eve*
2. Sylvester Stallone – *Rocky*
3. Gary Cooper – *Pride of the Yankees*
4. Marlon Brando – *On The Waterfront*
5. James Cagney – *Yankee Doodle Dandy*
6. Dustin Hoffman – *The Graduate*
7. Clint Eastwood – *Sudden Impact*
8. Edward G. Robinson – *Little Caesar*
9. Sean Connery – *Goldfinger*
10. Oliver Hardy – many Laurel and Hardy movies

Quiz #51 *(from page 69)*

1. "I want to be alone!"
2. Leo Gorcey
3. Betty Grable
4. Dean Martin
5. He was a dancer.
6. Clark Gable
7. Jimmy Lydon
8. Ma and Pa Kettle
9. Paul Whiteman
10. Robert Alda

Quiz #52 *(from page 71)*

1. d
2. j
3. f
4. a
5. b
6. h
7. g
8. i
9. e
10. c

Quiz #53 *(from page 73)*

1. *BUtterfield 8* (1960)
2. *Who's Afraid of Virginia Woolf?* (1966)
3. Violet
4. London, England
5. Conrad "Nicky" Hilton
6. Eleven years old
7. Eddie Fisher
8. *Cleopatra*
9. *The Little Foxes* (1982)
10. Richard Burton

Quiz #54 *(from page 74)*

1. j
2. i
3. h
4. f
5. g
6. e
7. d
8. c
9. b
10. a

Quiz #55 *(from page 75)*

1. Bogey
2. Baby
3. Hoppy
4. Uncle Milty
5. Dodo
6. C. B.
7. Babe
8. Red
9. Angie and Cat Woman
10. Gabby

Quiz #56 *(from page 76)*

1. b
2. c
3. a
4. b
5. a
6. all three
7. b
8. c
9. a
10. a

Quiz #57 *(from page 77)*
1. h
2. a
3. i
4. f
5. b
6. j
7. d
8. e
9. g
10. c

Quiz #58 *(from page 79)*
1. Ian Fleming
2. *Dr. No*
3. Ursula Andress
4. Roger Moore (7 films)
5. 22 movies
6. Sean Connery (6'3")
7. Daniel Craig (5'10")
8. Jaws
9. Shaken, not stirred
10. Roger Moore

Quiz #59 *(from page 80)*
1. True
2. True
3. False (She won it for *Kitty Foyle*.)
4. True
5. False (It was Lana Turner.)
6. True
7. False (It was William Randolph Hearst.)
8. False (It was Joe E. Lewis.)
9. True
10. False (It was *Pillow Talk*.)

Quiz #60 *(from page 81)*
1. h
2. c
3. f
4. b
5. j
6. g
7. e
8. d
9. i
10. a

Quiz #61 *(from page 83)*
1. True
2. False (She was 16.)
3. True
4. False (The role of Minnesota Fats was played by Jackie Gleason.)
5. False (It was the life story of Gus Kahn.)
6. False
7. True
8. True
9. False (Rosebud was a sled.)
10. True

Quiz #62 *(from page 84)*
1. c
2. g
3. h
4. a
5. d
6. i
7. j
8. f
9. b
10. e

Quiz #63 *(from page 85)*
1. Camp Crystal Lake
2. Balboa
3. *Around the World in 80 Days*
4. Four
5. Diana Ross
6. *Beach Party* (1963)
7. New York Knights
8. *Dirty Harry*
9. Raymond Massey
10. The real name of Samuel Goldwyn

Quiz #64 *(from page 87)*
1. *Snow White and the Seven Dwarfs*
2. *Pinocchio*
3. Donald Duck
4. 1955
5. *Steamboat Willie*
6. Jimmie Dodd
7. Mortimer Mouse
8. Doc, Bashful, Grumpy, Happy, Sleepy, Sneezy, and Dopey
9. The voice of Snow White
10. *Treasure Island*

Quiz #65 *(from page 88)*
1. c
2. g
3. h
4. d
5. a
6. j
7. i
8. b
9. f
10. e

Quiz #66 *(from page 89)*

1. Marlon Brando – *A Streetcar Named Desire*
2. Orson Welles – *Citizen Kane*
3. Robert DeNiro – *Tax Driver*
4. Danny Kaye – *The Court Jester*
5. Margaret Hamilton – *The Wizard of Oz*
6. Faye Dunaway – *Mommie Dearest*
7. Robert Armstrong – *King Kong*
8. Brandon De Wilde – *Shane*
9. Tony Curtis – *Spartacus*
10. Anthony Perkins – *Psycho*

Quiz #67 *(from page 91)*

1. c
2. c
3. c
4. b
5. a
6. a
7. c
8. a
9. c
10. a

Quiz #68 *(from page 93)*

1. Westport, Connecticut
2. The Navy in World War II
3. *The Color of Money*
4. *Cat On a Hot Tin Roof*
5. Auto racing
6. The Hole In the Wall Camp
7. *The Verdict*
8. A pink Cadillac
9. *Butch Cassidy and the Sundance Kid* and *The Sting*
10. *Slapshot*

Quiz #69 *(from page 94)*

1. d
2. f
3. h
4. a
5. j
6. c
7. b
8. i
9. g
10. e

Quiz #70 *(from page 95)*

1. *The Country Girl* and *High Society*
2. They have both been knighted.
3. Monumental Pictures
4. Anthony Hopkins
5. A lion roaring
6. Callahan
7. Boston Blackie
8. Betty Grable
9. Isaac Hayes
10. Citizen Kane

Quiz #71 *(from page 97)*

1. Harvard University
2. *Save the Tiger*
3. *Mister Roberts*
4. Six times
5. Walter Matthau
6. *Days of Wine and Roses*
7. Ricky Nelson
8. *Tuesdays With Morrie*
9. *Kotch*
10. *The Apartment*

Quiz #72 *(from page 99)*

1. g
2. c
3. h
4. j
5. a
6. b
7. e
8. i
9. f
10. d

About the Author

MEL SIMONS has amassed one of the world's largest old-time radio and television show collections. His knowledge of vintage entertainment is on display in his acclaimed books and lectures on the subject. Mel lives in Boston and can be heard on WBZ Radio.

More from Mel Simons!

More Trivia • More Memories • More Fun!

 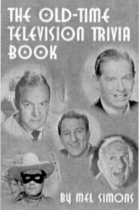 

 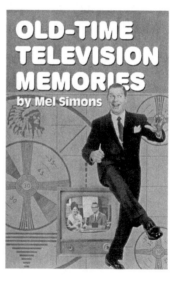

All only $14.95 each
Remember those golden years and order today!

Breinigsville, PA USA
01 December 2010

250455BV00005B/16/P